Celebrating Hockey's History

The Original 6

MONTREAL CANADIENS

Eric Zweig

Crabtree Publishing Company

www.crabtreebooks.com

Celebrating Hockey's History
The Original 6

Author: Eric Zweig,
  Member of the Society for International
  Hockey Research

Editor: Ellen Rodger

Editorial director: Kathy Middleton

Design: Tammy McGarr

Photo research: Tammy McGarr

Proofreader: Wendy Scavuzzo

**Production coordinator and
  Prepress technician:** Tammy McGarr

Print coordinator: Margaret Amy Salter

Photo Credits:
AP Images: Philippe Bouchard/Cal Sport Medi, p 28
CP Images: p 12; STRGHS, p 15 (top right); 16–17 (top middle);
Getty Images: Bettmann, pp 15 (bottom), 19; B Bennett, p23 (middle and
  bottom right); Denis Brodeur , p25 (top); Toronto Star Archives, p29
Hockey Hall of Fame: Lewis Portnoy, pp 18 (bottom right); 21 (bottom
  left), 26 (middle and bottom right);
Icon Sportswire: David Kirouac, front cover, title page; IHA, p 23 (top left);
  Cliff Welch, p 23 (bottom middle
Shutterstock: © meunierd, pp 11, 17 (bottom left);
Wikimedia: Quist, p 4; creative commons, pp 5 (top middle), 18 (bottom
  left); public domain, pp 5 (top left), 7 (bottom), 10, 14, 15 (top left), 17
  (top right and centre), p 18 (top left); 20, 21 (top left and middle), 23 (top
  right), 24, 26 (top left and right); William James Topley (1845–1930), p 5
  (top right); Hockey Hall of Fame / Library and Archives Canada / PA-
  049464, p 5 (bottom); Library and Archives Canada / Gazette collection, p
  6; Library and Archives Canada, p 7 (top right); Alex Goykhman, p 8; p 18
  (top right); Michael Miller, p 22; Erin Costa, p 26 (bottom left)

Library and Archives Canada Cataloguing in Publication

Zweig, Eric, 1963-, author
        Montreal Canadiens / Eric Zweig.

(The original six : celebrating hockey's history)
Includes index.
Issued in print and electronic formats.
ISBN 978-0-7787-3439-0 (hardcover).--
ISBN 978-0-7787-3445-1 (softcover).--
ISBN 978-1-4271-1924-7 (HTML)

        1. Montreal Canadiens (Hockey team)--Juvenile literature.
2. Montreal Canadiens (Hockey team)--History--Juvenile literature.I.
Title.

GV848.M6Z84 2017   j796.962'640971428   C2017-903481-2
                                                   C2017-903482-0

Library of Congress Cataloging-in-Publication Data

Names: Zweig, Eric, 1963- author.
Title: Montreal Canadiens / Eric Zweig.
Description: New York : Crabtree Publishing Company, [2018] |
  Series: The Original Six: Celebrating hockey's history |
  Includes index. | Audience: Ages: 10-14.
Identifiers: LCCN 2017029655 (print) | LCCN 2017039892 (ebook) |
  ISBN 9781427119247 (Electronic HTML) |
  ISBN 9780778734390 (Reinforced library binding) |
  ISBN 9780778734451 (Paperback)
Subjects: LCSH: Montreal Canadiens (Hockey team)--History--Juvenile
  literature.
Classification: LCC GV848.M6 (ebook) | LCC GV848.M6 Z94 2018 (print)
  | DDC 796.962/640971428--dc23
LC record available at https://lccn.loc.gov/2017029655

Crabtree Publishing Company

www.crabtreebooks.com   1-800-387-7650

Printed in the USA/102017/CG20170907

Published in Canada
Crabtree Publishing
616 Welland Ave.
St. Catharines, Ontario
L2M 5V6

Published in the United States
Crabtree Publishing
PMB 59051
350 Fifth Avenue, 59th Floor
New York, New York 10118

Published in the United Kingdom
Crabtree Publishing
Maritime House
Basin Road North, Hove
BN41 1WR

Published in Australia
Crabtree Publishing
3 Charles Street
Coburg North
VIC, 3058

Table of Contents

Celebrating Hockey's History

The Original 6

THE LEAGUE, THE HABS, THE CUP

For something so old, the National Hockey League sure moves fast! In fact, as the league marks its eleventh decade, the game on the ice is faster than ever. The top stars skate with blinding speed, and can fire the puck as though their sticks were launching rockets. Goalies need to react with lightning-fast **reflexes** to make a save.

Les Glorieux

The Montreal Canadiens are the NHL's greatest team. If you like to cheer for someone else, you might not think so. But throughout 100 years of NHL history, the numbers don't lie. The first NHL games were played on December 19, 1917. The Canadiens got their first win that night when they defeated the original Ottawa Senators 7–4. Since then, the Canadiens have scored more goals, won more games, and won the Stanley Cup more times than any other **franchise** in the NHL. They've also had many of the greatest players in hockey history in their lineup. No wonder fans call them *Les Glorieux*, meaning The Glorious!

A mural by Charles Pachter "Les Rois de l'Arène", (Kings of the Arena), 1984

Silky Mitts!

Joe Malone led the Montreal Canadiens with five goals in the team's first NHL game. He'd go on to lead the league with 44 goals in just 20 games played in 1917–18.

The NHL was formed in meetings at the Windsor Hotel in Montreal on November 22 and 26, 1917.

Canadiens goalie Georges Vezina recorded the first shutout in NHL history, beating the Toronto Maple Leafs 9–0 on February 18, 1918.

That Silver Cup

The history of hockey begins long before the NHL or the Montreal Canadiens. Games with balls and sticks have been popular since ancient times, and have been played on ice since at least the 1500s. Historians like to debate where hockey began, but the game truly caught on after it was moved inside, from frozen lakes and rivers, to the Victoria Rink in Montreal in 1875. Hockey's popularity really exploded after Canada's Governor-General, Lord Stanley of Preston, donated the Stanley Cup in 1893. The Governor-General is Canada's head of state. The Cup was won that year by the hockey club from the Montreal Amateur Athletic Association.

Lord Stanley

The Montreal Canadiens are actually older than the NHL, but they're not quite as old as the Stanley Cup. Their history begins during the winter of 1909–10 with the formation of a league known as the National Hockey Association.

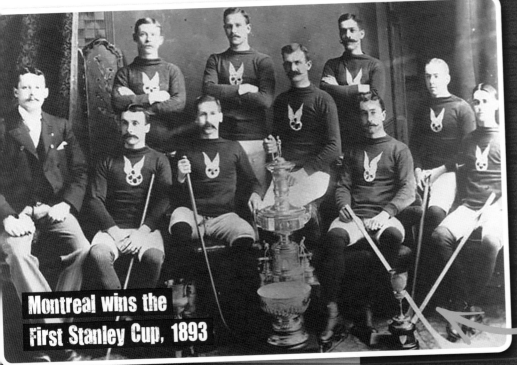

Montreal wins the First Stanley Cup, 1893

THE ORIGINALS

Five teams took part in the meetings that formed the NHL back in 1917. There was a team from Toronto, a team from Quebec City, a team from Ottawa, and two teams from Montreal: the Wanderers and the Canadiens. Quebec decided not to play during the first two seasons, so the NHL began with just four teams on the ice.

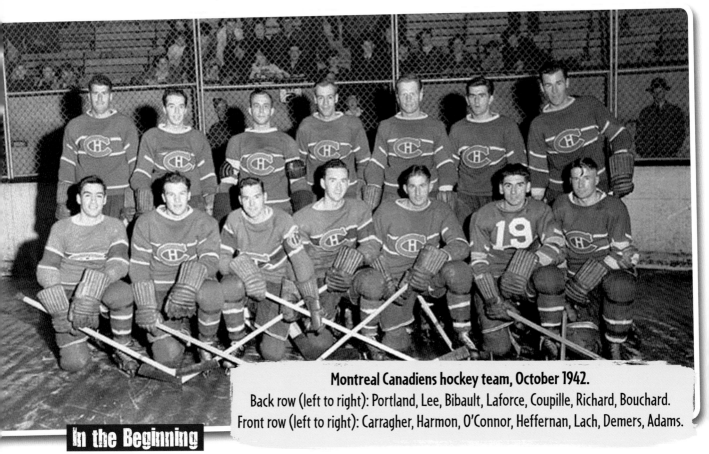

Montreal Canadiens hockey team, October 1942.
Back row (left to right): Portland, Lee, Bibault, Laforce, Coupille, Richard, Bouchard.
Front row (left to right): Carragher, Harmon, O'Connor, Heffernan, Lach, Demers, Adams.

In the Beginning

The NHL was born during tough times. Soldiers were still fighting World War I when the league began. Then, early in the first season of 1917–18, a fire destroyed the Montreal Arena and the Montreal Wanderers dropped out. The NHL was left with just three teams! That's a long way from the 31 teams that are in the league 100 years later. By the 1920s, people wanted to forget all about the war years. They wanted to have fun. Music got jazzier, movies began to feature talking actors, and sports fans flocked to stadiums and arenas to cheer for their favorite teams. The NHL was back up to four teams by its third season of 1919–20, and it continued to grow. Soon, the league had expanded beyond Canada, adding teams in United States, too. By the start of the 1926–27 season, there were 10 teams in the NHL.

Surviving During Tough Times

Then times got tough again. The **stock market** crashed in 1929, plunging the world into an economic disaster known as the **Great Depression**. Businesses closed. People were out of work. Sports teams had a hard time drawing fans. NHL teams in Ottawa and Pittsburgh moved to new cities, but it made no difference. Both soon dropped out of the NHL. During the good times, another new team had been added in Montreal. It was known as the Montreal Maroons. During the 1930s, even a city as crazy about hockey as Montreal couldn't support two teams. The Maroons folded, but the Canadiens survived.

Soup kitchens were opened to feed the hungry during the Depression. With work scarce, people didn't have money for food, let alone extras such as sports tickets.

The Original Six

By the start of the 1942–43 season, the Canadiens were one of just six teams left in the NHL. The others were the Toronto Maple Leafs, the Boston Bruins, the New York Rangers, the Detroit Red Wings, and the Chicago Black Hawks (now the Blackhawks). These were the only teams in the NHL for 25 seasons, until the league began to expand again in 1967. They are often referred to as "The Original Six."

Toronto Maple Leafs

Boston Bruins

New York Rangers

Detroit Red Wings

Montreal Canadiens

Chicago Black Hawks
(now Blackhawks)

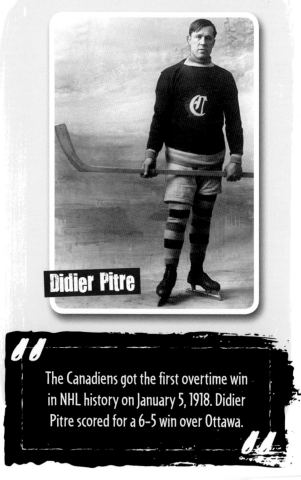

Didier Pitre

" The Canadiens got the first overtime win in NHL history on January 5, 1918. Didier Pitre scored for a 6–5 win over Ottawa. "

THE STANLEY CUP

Original Bowl

First awarded in 1893!
Players like to drink out of this

The Montreal Wanderers became the first team to engrave player names on the Stanley Cup in 1907.

Every Stanley Cup winning team has engraved player names on the trophy since the Montreal Canadiens' victory in **1924**.

In **1993**, the Cup celebrated **100** years.

Guess who won it that year? Here's a clue:

_ _ _ _ t _ _ a _
_ _ _ _ _ d _ e _ _

The Canadiens have made it to the Stanley Cup final a record 34 times.

Detachable Rings

* When there is no more space left, the oldest ring is removed and retired. It stays at the Hockey Hall of Fame.

* A new ring is placed on the bottom for new winning teams and players.

* Winner names remain on the cup for roughly 50 years before the ring is retired.

The Canadiens reached the Stanley Cup Finals for **10** straight seasons from **1950-51** through **1959-60**. They set a record by winning the cup **5** years in a row from **1956 to 1960**.

The Stanley Cup weighs a whopping **34.5 pounds (15.5 kg)** – What does hefting the cup feel like?

6 full grown chihuahuas

Their cup overfloweth!

Montreal has claimed the cup a record 24 times!

Montreal's Stanley Cup Wins

Year	Team
1993	Los Angeles Kings
1986	Calgary Flames
1979	New York Rangers
1978	Boston Bruins
1977	Boston Bruins
1976	Philadelphia Flyers
1973	Chicago Black Hawks
1971	Chicago Black Hawks
1969	St. Louis Blues
1968	St. Louis Blues
1966	Detroit Red Wings
1965	Chicago Black Hawks
1960	Toronto Maple Leafs
1959	Toronto Maple Leafs
1958	Boston Bruins
1957	Boston Bruins
1956	Detroit Red Wings
1953	Boston Bruins
1946	Boston Bruins
1944	Chicago Black Hawks
1931	Chicago Black Hawks
1930	Boston Bruins
1924	Calgary Tigers
1916	Portland Rosebuds

The Canadiens were still members of the National Hockey Association when they won their first Stanley Cup in 1916. They defeated Portland of the Pacific Coast Hockey Association (PCHA) to win it.

11 Henri Richard's name on the cup

(all as a Canadiens player, with 5 consecutive years from 1956 to 1960.)

11 Toe Blake's name on the cup

(8x as a Canadienss coach, 2x as a Canadiens player, and 1 time as a player with the Montreal Maroons.)

17 Jean Beliveau's name on the cup

(10x as a Canadiens player and 7 as a team executive.)

Whoops!

Canadiens players forgot the Stanley Cup by the side of the road after changing a flat tire on their car en route to a team party in 1924. They later found the cup exactly where they had left it!

Felled by the Flu

The 1919 Stanley Cup was cancelled because of the deadly Spanish flu. The series pitted the Canadiens against the Seattle Metropolitans of the PCHA. After five games with two wins and a tie for each team, the series was cancelled. Most of the Canadiens players were sick, including team owner George Kennedy and star player Joe Hall. Hall died four days later.

We Shall Call Him Stanley!

Goaltender Georges Vezina's wife gave birth to a baby boy the day after Montreal's 1916 cup victory. Though the child was named Joseph Louis Marcel Vezina, everyone called him Stanley.

The Canadiens won a record 10 playoff games in overtime leading up to their 1993 cup win.

THE FLYING FRENCHMEN

The Montreal Canadiens were founded on December 4, 1909. They were one of five charter, or first, members of the brand new National Hockey Association. During their first two seasons, the Canadiens could only have French Canadian players on their roster. Today, their players come from all around the world.

The 1912-13 NHA season Montreal Canadiens team with their canine mascot.

And the Name Stuck

The earliest stars of the Montreal Canadiens were "Newsy" Lalonde, Jack Laviolette, and Didier Pitre. These three players were so fast and so skillful that people called them "The Flying Frenchmen." Soon, the nickname was used to describe the entire team.

The Stratford Streak

The Canadiens' first new superstar in the NHL joined the team for the 1923–24 season. His name was Howie Morenz. He was born in the tiny town of Mitchell, Ontario, and grew up in nearby Stratford. Morenz wasn't a "Frenchman," but he sure could fly! With his blazing speed, Morenz was known as "The Canadien Comet," "The Mitchell Meteor," and "The Stratford Streak." He quickly became the top scorer in the NHL, and he led the Canadiens to Stanley Cup championships in 1924, 1930, and 1931.

During his career, Howie Morenz set NHL career records with 271 goals and 472 points.

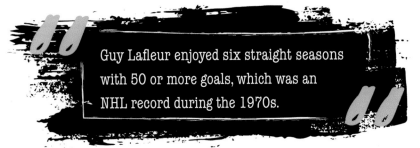

Guy Lafleur enjoyed six straight seasons with 50 or more goals, which was an NHL record during the 1970s.

The Rocket Era

After 1931, the Canadiens didn't win the Stanley Cup again until the 1943–44 season. By then, they were led by a new young superstar who'd grown up in Montreal. Maurice Richard wasn't the most talented player, but he had a knack for putting the puck in the net. With his explosive scoring skill, he was soon known as "The Rocket." In his 18 seasons with the Canadiens from 1942 to 1960, Richard helped Montreal win the Stanley Cup eight times.

During his career, Maurice Richard set NHL career records with 544 goals and 946 points.

More Championships

Jean Beliveau became captain of the Canadiens in 1961–62, and he made sure the championships continued. Montreal enjoyed five more Stanley Cup wins before Beliveau retired in 1971. That year, the Canadiens made Guy Lafleur the number-one pick in the NHL Draft. Lafleur became the next great Flying Frenchman. Montreal crowds leaped to their feet to cheer him when he flew up the ice with his blond hair blowing in the breeze behind him. Lafleur was the NHL's top scorer for three straight seasons in the 1970s, and helped Montreal win the Stanley Cup five more times.

Jean Beliveau played 20 seasons with the Montreal Canadiens— a team record he shares with Maurice Richard's brother Henri Richard.

Habs History

H is for **Habitant**... well, not quite. That's hockey lore, popularized in 1926 by the owner of the New York Rangers, Tex Rickard. Habitant refers to the French settlers of Quebec. It was used as a nickname for the Canadiens as early as 1914. However the H actually stands for hockey, as in the team's name: Club de Hockey Canadien.

The Canadiens set an NHL record that still stands with 132 points in the standings in 1976–77.

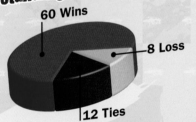

60 Wins
8 Loss
12 Ties

Their record during the 80-game season was 60-8-12.

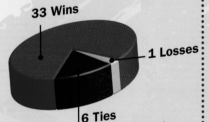

33 Wins
1 Losses
6 Ties

Montreal was almost unbeatable in their own rink that season, posting a home record of 33-1-6.

The Montreal Canadiens celebrate their Stanley Cup win over the Detroit Red Wings in 1966. Coach Toe Blake grabs the front of the cup. Team captain Jean Beliveau smiles above the cup.

Canadiens Regular-Season Franchise Leaders (Season)

GOALS: Steve Shutt – **60** (1976–77)

Guy Lafleur – **60** (1977–78)

ASSISTS: Pete Mahovlich – **82** (1974–75)

POINTS: Guy Lafleur – **136** (1976–77)

WINS: Carey Price – **44** (2014–15)

SHUTOUTS: George Hainsworth – **22** (1928–29)

AVERAGE: George Hainsworth – **0.92** (1928–29)

Canadiens Regular-Season Franchise Leaders (Career)

GAMES: Henri Richard – **1,256**

GOALS: Maurice Richard – **544**

ASSISTS: Guy Lafleur – **728**

POINTS: Guy Lafleur – **1,246**

WINS: Jacques Plante – **314**

SHUTOUTS: George Hainsworth – **75**

AVERAGE: George Hainsworth – **1.78**

Hanging in the Rafters

The Canadiens have retired quite a few jerseys over the years. Retired numbers cannot be used again, meaning Habs players are now inching into the high numbers.

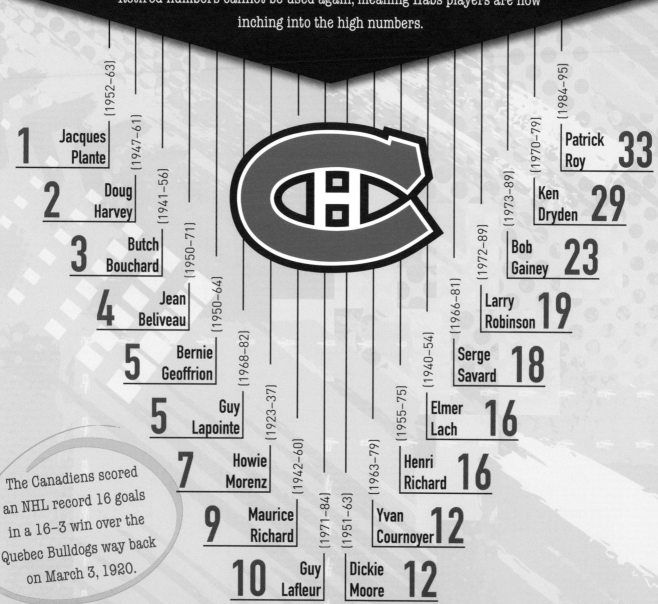

1 Jacques Plante (1952–63)

2 Doug Harvey (1947–61)

3 Butch Bouchard (1941–56)

4 Jean Beliveau (1950–71)

5 Bernie Geoffrion (1950–64)

5 Guy Lapointe (1968–82)

7 Howie Morenz (1923–37)

9 Maurice Richard (1942–60)

10 Guy Lafleur (1971–84)

12 Dickie Moore (1951–63)

12 Yvan Cournoyer (1963–79)

16 Henri Richard (1955–75)

16 Elmer Lach (1940–54)

18 Serge Savard (1966–81)

19 Larry Robinson (1972–89)

23 Bob Gainey (1973–89)

29 Ken Dryden (1970–79)

33 Patrick Roy (1984–95)

The Canadiens scored an NHL record 16 goals in a 16–3 win over the Quebec Bulldogs way back on March 3, 1920.

First Canadiens Game
Date: **1/5/1910**
Score: **7–6**
(a win against the Cobalt Silver Kings)

So Nice, They Played It Twice

The National Hockey Association added two new teams in 1910 and the season started over. So the first **official** Canadiens game was the second one.

But Also
Date: **1/19/1910**
Score: **9–4**
(a loss against the Renfrew Millionaires)

Le Bleu, Blanc, et Rouge

A lot of sports teams change their uniforms every few seasons. New logos and new colors can help make a team more popular. It can certainly help them sell more hats and jerseys to their fans. Yet some teams rarely change the things they wear. Their looks are **iconic**. That certainly describes the Montreal Canadiens.

La Sante-Flanelle

When the Canadiens started out in 1909–10, the team wore light blue sweaters. The next season, the main color changed to red, with a green maple leaf on the chest and a fancy white "C" inside it. By 1911–12 blue, white, and red became the team's colors, and they have remained "le tricolore" ever since. In fact, le tricolore and le bleu-blanc-rouge are two of the team's many nicknames! The others are: the Habs (for Habitants, of course), Les Glorieux, Le Grand Club, La Sante-Flanelle, Le Canadiens, and Le CH. La Sante-Flanelle, or "the holy flannel" is a reference to the **revered** status of the club's sweater, or jersey, and the almost religious devotion of the fans.

Mid-1940's Montreal Canadiens.

Sweet Sweaters

By the 1915–16 season, the Canadiens were wearing sweaters (yes, wool sweaters) that didn't look very different from the ones the team still wears today. Except today, they are high-tech jerseys that wick sweat away. In 1915–16, the scratchy sweaters had a CA logo, which stands for the Club Athletique Canadiens instead of the CH logo, for the team's name, Club de Hockey Canadien, introduced in 1916–17.

Hey You!

Players' names were added to the back of the Canadiens jerseys for the first time during the playoffs in 1977. They've been a permanent fixture since the 1977–78 season.

For many years, the Canadiens jersey was the favorite for young hockey fans and players in Quebec. In the book *The Hockey Sweater*, Canadian author Roch Carrier wrote about being mistakenly sent a Toronto Maple Leafs jersey as a child and the **humiliation** of having to wear it.

Dwight King

Bigger, Bulkier

Although the uniforms haven't changed much over the years, the players wearing them sure look different. Most players today are a lot bigger and stronger than they used to be. They wear equipment made from modern materials that allow their padding to be bigger and stronger, too, even though it's much lighter than old-fashioned equipment made from leather and felt. They also wear helmets with visors, and guards to their necks, shins, and mouth. Even with the helmets, and face-saving visors and mouthguards, cuts, bruises, and losing teeth are a normal part of the game.

Jacques Plante's Mask

In the old days, goalies got it the worst. They didn't wear masks, so smashed cheekbones and cuts that required stitches were common. Canadiens goalie Jacques Plante changed all that. After suffering a serious cut on his face in a game on November 1, 1959, Plante wouldn't return to the net without using the mask he'd been wearing in practice. Plante played so well while wearing his mask that goalies on other teams started wearing them, too.

ON HOME ICE

Bricks and mortar, wood and cement... Some hockey arenas are just buildings but the Montreal Forum was a temple of hockey history.

Forum Figures

$1.5 million
the cost of construction
(equivalent to about
$21 million today)

1924—the year the Forum opened

159—the number of days it took to
build the Forum

9,300—the original seating capacity

18,200—the seating capacity in the
Forum by the 1968–69 season

1996—the year the Canadiens
moved out of the Forum

1997—the year the Forum was declared a
National Historic Site of Canada

Before the Forum, the Canadiens played at Westmount Arena from 1910 to 1918, and at Mount Royal Arena from 1920 to 1926.

Forum Facts

- It became the Canadiens permanent home in 1926–27. The Canadiens shared the Forum with the Montreal Maroons until the Maroons folded in 1938.

- When Montreal hosted the 1976 Summer Olympics, gymnastics was held at the Forum. So were the finals for basketball, volleyball, handball, and boxing.

- The Canadiens played their final game at the Montreal Forum on March 11, 1996. They beat the Dallas Stars 4–1.

- Legendary British band The Beatles once played the Forum in 1964.

- Today, the Forum is an entertainment complex with theaters, shops, and restaurants. There is a spot marking center ice and some of the original seats are used as benches throughout the building.

- Fans had a chance to buy old Forum seats in an auction held after the Forum closed.

Center Ice Send Off

The Forum was the scene of the March 11, 1937, funeral for Howie Morenz. The Canadiens star had suffered a badly broken leg during a January 28 game against Chicago. The rumor was that, realizing his career was over, Morenz died of a broken heart. In reality, the leg was set, but Morenz died March 8, when blood clots led to an **embolism**. More than 10,000 people attended the funeral for the player with heart, while more than 200,000 people lined the streets outside to pay their last respects.

Howie Morenz

The Bell Centre

It was originally called Molson Centre when the Canadiens played their first game there on March 16, 1993. They beat the Rangers 4–2. The name changed to Bell Centre in 2002.

Bell Centre Figures

$270 million	cost of construction
1993–1996	years under construction
21,288	seating capacity—the largest for a North American hockey arena

HABS HEROES

During the 1940s and 1950s, French Canadians in Montreal often felt like second-class citizens in their own city. English businesses dominated Montreal, and English was the main language spoken in the city. With their great success on the ice, the many great stars of the Montreal Canadiens became huge hometown heroes. The biggest hero of all was Maurice Richard.

The Rocket

Maurice Richard overcame serious injuries early in his career to become a legendary goal-scorer. He soon became the first player in NHL history to score 50 goals in a single season. He did it in just 50 games played in 1944–45! He went on to become the first player in NHL history to score 500 goals in his career. In 1999, the Canadiens donated the Maurice Richard Trophy to the NHL to reward the top goal-scorer each season.

Boom Boom

Bernie Geoffrion grew up in Montreal dreaming of playing with the Canadiens. In his first full season with the team in 1950–51, he won the Calder Trophy as NHL rookie of the year. He went on to win two scoring titles and became the second player in NHL history to score 50 goals in 1961–62. Geoffrion's slap shot was so powerful, that he earned the nickname "Boom Boom."

Le Gros Bill (Big Bill)

Nicknamed for a character in a French-Canadian folk song, Jean Beliveau was tall and strong, yet speedy and graceful. "Classy" is the best word to describe Beliveau. The Canadiens wanted him so badly in the early 1950s they supposedly convinced the entire Quebec Senior Hockey League to turn professional in order to obtain his rights. Beliveau led the NHL in scoring in 1955–56 and won the Hart Trophy as most valuable player (MVP) twice. He always said his proudest moment was when his teammates voted him captain of the Canadiens in 1961.

Le Capitaine (The Captain)

Bob Gainey was never a great goal scorer, but he had other talents that made him very valuable. Gainey was a strong checker who could shut down other teams' top stars. In 1976, legendary Russian coach Viktor Tikhonov called Gainey the most technically perfect hockey player in the world. When the NHL created the Selke Trophy in 1977 to honor the league's best defensive forward, Gainey won it four years in a row.

Maurice Richard (left), Guy Lafleur (center) and Bernie Geoffrion (right) are the first three members of the Montreal Canadiens to have scored 50 or more goals during the regular season.

Since 1952, the Montreal Canadiens have had two lines of John McCrae's World War I poem, "In Flanders Fields," posted on their dressing room wall for inspiration. "To you from failing hands we throw the torch; be yours to hold it high." It means that every generation of new, young players must never forget the greatness of the past.

Carey Price

GREAT GOALIES

When he's healthy and on his game, many people feel that Carey Price is the greatest goalie in hockey today. It's often been said that you can't win without a great goalie, and the Montreal Canadiens have boasted some of the greatest in hockey history.

The Chicoutimi Cucumber

Georges Vezina joined the Canadiens for their second season in 1910–11. Over the next 15 years, he never missed a single game! He played 328 straight in the regular season, plus another 39 in the playoffs. In the NHA, goalies weren't allowed to drop to the ice to make saves, and even when the NHL changed the rules, Vezina almost always played standing up. His great career ended on November 28, 1925, when he collapsed during the first game of the NHL season. Vezina had tuberculosis, a serious lung disease. He died on March 27, 1926. To honor his memory, the Canadiens donated the Vezina Trophy to the NHL. It has gone to the league's best goalie ever since the 1926–27 season.

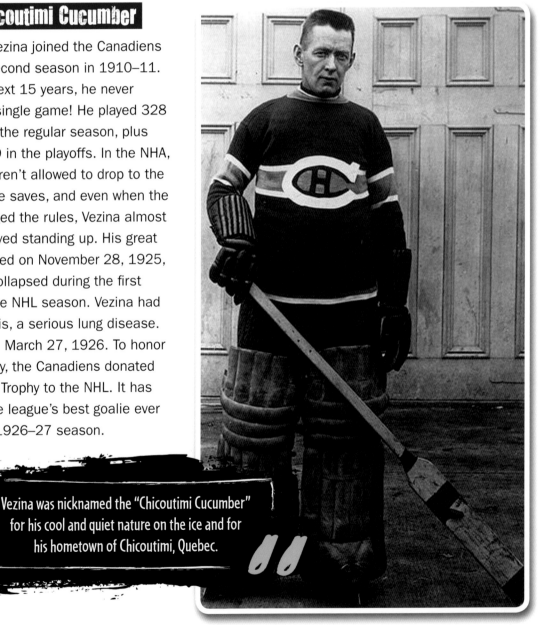

" Vezina was nicknamed the "Chicoutimi Cucumber" for his cool and quiet nature on the ice and for his hometown of Chicoutimi, Quebec. "

Vezina's Replacement

George Hainsworth joined the Canadiens in 1926–27. He was the winner of the Vezina Trophy the first three years it was presented. There wasn't a lot of offense in the NHL in that era. All goalies put up spectacular numbers, but nobody's were as amazing as Hainsworth's. During the 1928–29 season, he set two NHL records that will likely stand forever. Hainsworth had 22 shutouts during the 44-game schedule and allowed only 43 goals for an average of 0.92. Starting the next season, the NHL introduced more modern passing rules to help increase the offense.

Short, But Sweet

Bill Durnan had a short career, but it was pretty spectacular. Durnan only played in the NHL for seven seasons with Montreal, from 1943–44 to 1949–50. But he won the Vezina Trophy six times! He was ambidextrous, meaning he used his left and right hands equally well. Durnan wore special gloves so that he could hold his stick with either hand. The only goalie to win the Vezina Trophy more times than Durnan is Jacques Plante. Plante won it six times with the Canadiens from 1956 to 1962 and won it for the seventh time with the St. Louis Blues in 1968–69.

Cup Clincher

Ken Dryden also had a short career, but he was long on results! In just eight seasons from 1971 to 1979, Dryden led the NHL in wins four times, he won the Vezina Trophy five times, and he helped the Canadiens win the Stanley Cup six times.

5 Vezina Trophy

6 Stanley Cup

TROPHY WINNERS

Hockey is a team game, and the Stanley Cup is the ultimate team prize. Still, there are plenty of impressive individual awards for NHL players to win. Here's the scoop on some Canadiens players who've won major individual awards.

The **Hart Trophy** is the NHL's oldest award. It's given to the player judged most valuable to his team, so it's also the most important individual trophy.

Donated to the NHL in 1924 by Dr. David Hart. His son, Cecil Hart, was a Montreal sports executive who was coach and general manager of the Canadiens in the 1920s and 1930s.

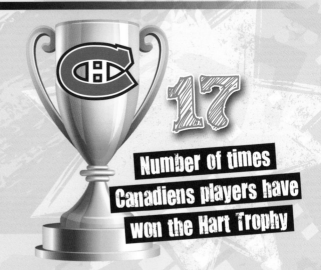

17 Number of times Canadiens players have won the Hart Trophy

Multiple winners

3 **Howie Morenz** (1927–28, 1930–31, 1931–32)

2 **Jean Beliveau** (1955–56, 1963–64)

2 **Guy Lafleur** (1976–77, 1977–78)

There was a 37-year gap in Montreal player Hart Trophy awards from Lafleur's 1977–78 award until Carey Price's in 2014–15.

Only seven goalies have ever won the Hart Trophy, and three of them played for the Canadiens. Jacques Plante won it in 1962. José Théodore won it in 2002. Carey Price won it in 2015.

Carey Price

The **Art Ross Trophy** has been given to the NHL's scoring leader since the 1947–48 season. The first winner was Montreal's **Elmer Lach**.

Maurice Richard led the NHL in goal-scoring five times in his career, but he never led the league in points so he never won the Art Ross Trophy. Great as he was, the only individual award Richard ever won was the **Hart Trophy** in 1947.

Ken Dryden played just six games for the Montreal Canadiens late in the 1970–71 season, but the team decided to use him as their starting goalie in the playoffs. He led Montreal to the Stanley Cup and won the **Conn Smythe Trophy** as playoff MVP that season. Officially, Dryden was still a rookie in 1971–72 and he won the **Calder Trophy** that season as rookie of the year.

Three-Timer

Goalie **Patrick Roy** led the Canadiens to the Stanley Cup as a rookie in 1985–86. He won the **Conn Smythe Trophy** as playoff MVP that year, then won it again when the Canadiens took the cup in 1993. When Roy won it again with the Colorado Avalanche in 2001, he became the only **three-time** winner of the Conn Smythe Trophy.

Montreal's **Doug Harvey** won the **Norris Trophy** as the NHL's best defenseman five times in six years from 1954 to 1961. He won it for the sixth time in 1962 while playing for the New York Rangers. Only Bobby Orr, who won the Norris eight times with the Boston Bruins, has been named the NHL's top **blueliner** more times than Harvey.

BEHIND THE BENCH

When a team struggles, you'll often hear somebody say that it's easier to fire one coach than 20 players. Still, a successful coach can stick around for a very long time. Between 1940 and 1980, just three men coached the Montreal Canadiens for 35 of those 40 years. All three rank among the greatest coaches in hockey history.

ALL-TIME GREATS

DICK IRVIN

Irvin and Blake

Dick Irvin was a star player in other leagues before joining the NHL in 1926. He became the coach of the Maple Leafs in 1931 and helped turn Toronto into an NHL powerhouse. In 1940, he left Toronto for Montreal. The Canadiens were struggling at the time, but Irvin quickly turned them around. He led Montreal to Stanley Cup wins in 1944, 1946, and 1953. Irvin spent 15 seasons as coach of the Canadiens. That's longer than anyone else in the team's history! When Montreal replaced him in 1955–56, they brought in a former star who'd been captain of the team under Irvin. Toe Blake coached the Canadiens for the next 12 seasons and Montreal never missed the playoffs. He retired in 1968 after leading the Canadiens to the Stanley Cup for the eighth time!

Scotty Bowman

Unlike Dick Irvin and Toe Blake, Scotty Bowman was not a star player. He suffered a head injury in junior hockey, and though he played another two years after that, he was never the same again. So he got into coaching. Bowman became a coach in the Canadiens **farm system** in the late 1950s. He made it to the NHL with the St. Louis Blues in 1967, then returned to Montreal to coach the Canadiens at the start of the 1971–72 season. Bowman worked his players hard, and although they didn't always like him, he always got the best out of them. In eight seasons, Bowman's team averaged more than 50 wins per year! They won the Stanley Cup five times. In all, Bowman coached in the NHL for 30 years with five different teams. He won a record 1,244 games in the regular season and broke Toe Blake's Stanley Cup record by winning nine championships.

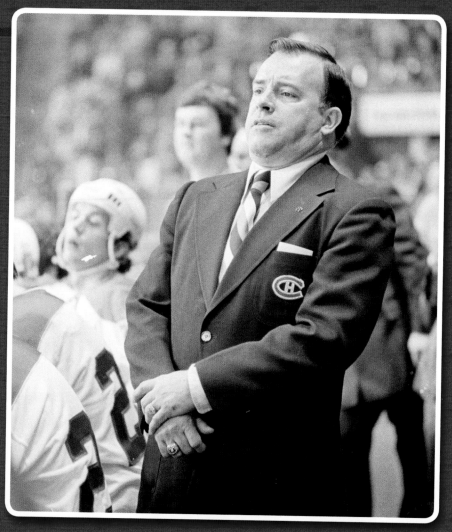

The Old Switcheroo!

During the 2002–03 season, the Canadiens fired coach Michel Therrien and replaced him with Claude Julien. Therrien became coach of the Canadiens again in 2012–13, but was fired midway through the 2016–17 season. His replacement? Claude Julien!

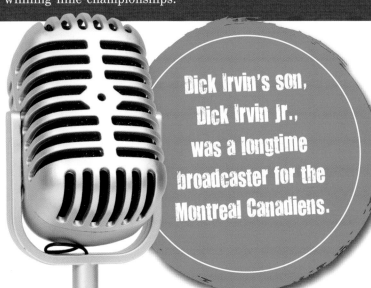

Dick Irvin's son, Dick Irvin Jr., was a longtime broadcaster for the Montreal Canadiens.

FAN FUN FACTS

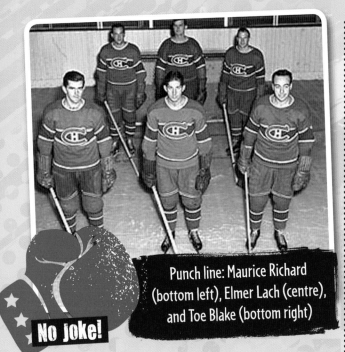

Punch line: Maurice Richard (bottom left), Elmer Lach (centre), and Toe Blake (bottom right)

No joke!

During the mid 1940s, the Canadiens' combination of Elmer Lach centering Toe Blake and Maurice Richard was the NHL's top-scoring line. Together, they were known as "The Punch Line." They sure provided plenty of offensive punch!

The Rocket

The Pocket Rocket

The Vest Pocket Rocket

Brothers in Arms

With his big brother Maurice, known as "The Rocket," fans took to calling little brother Henri Richard "The Pocket Rocket." Another brother, Claude Richard, never made it past the minors, but he was known as "The Vest Pocket Rocket."

Montreal Canadiens Flow Chart

"Flow" is a slang term in hockey circles for hair that flows well in and out of a helmet. Throughout their history, the Canadiens have had some league leaders in fantastic flow.

Maurice Richard

Maurice Richard had a full head of carefully coifed hair.

Guy Lafleur

Guy Lafleur's famous flowing golden locks were even depicted on his Bell Centre statue.

Larry Robinson

Larry Robinson was famous for his curly locks and sideburns that were so massive, they too had flow.

Jordie Benn

Most players sport scruff for the playoffs, but Jordie Benn's beard was year-round lumberjack-level.

Nickname Game

Nicknames are a time-honored hockey tradition. Montreal players past and present have some of the best in the league.

Toe Toe Blake's real first name was Hector. His little brother couldn't pronounce his name properly, and it came out like Hec-toe. Soon the family starting calling him "Toe".

Roadrunner Yvan Cournoyer starred with the Canadiens from 1963 to 1979. He was so fast on the ice that he was nicknamed "The Roadrunner" after the cartoon bird.

Big Bird Because of his size and his bushy blond hair, Canadiens defenseman Larry Robinson was known as "Big Bird" like the Sesame Street character. Robinson anchored the Montreal defense in the 1970s along with Serge Savard and Guy Lapointe. Together, they were known as "The Big Three."

The Flower Guy Lafleur was known as "The Flower" because that's what his last name means in English. He was also known as "Le Demon Blond" (The Blond Demon).

Bionic Blueberry Mario Tremblay was given the nickname "Bleuet Bionique" because he came from Lac-Saint-Jean, an area of Quebec known for growing the best blueberries. Tremblay was known for his speed and skill on the ice that seemed robotically efficient.

Boom Boom Geoffrion Bernard "Bernie" Geoffrion was known for his booming slap shot and hard, physical play. He broke his nose six times during his career.

Gump A player whose nickname is so well known that fans might not recognize his given name, Lorne "Gump" Worsley played for Montreal through four Stanley Cups (1965, 1966, 1968, 1969). He earned the nickname Gump because he looked like comic-strip character, Andy Gump.

The Senator The first defenseman in NHL history to win the Conn Smythe Trophy, Serge Savard was also given the nicknames "The Senator" for his interest in politics and "Minister of Defense" for his commanding play.

Their names sound like cartoon characters, but brothers Sprague and Odie Cleghorn were two of the best players in hockey in the early days of the NHL. Odie was a high-scoring forward and Sprague was a top defenseman. They played together with the Canadiens from 1921–22 to 1924–25.

Numbers Game

1957–58 and 1958–59

Dickie Moore won the Art Ross Trophy as the NHL scoring leader in back-to-back seasons. He accomplished the feat the first time despite playing the final three months of the season with a cast on his arm to protect a broken wrist.

18 years + 75 days old

Mario Tremblay is the youngest player to score a goal for the Canadiens (November 16, 1974).

41 years + 177 days old

George Hainsworth is the oldest player in Canadiens history. He played his final game for Montreal in 1937.

11/ 22/ 2003

The Canadiens played in the NHL's first outdoor game, beating the Edmonton Oilers 4–3 at Commonwealth Stadium in Edmonton. Despite a temperature of –0.4 °F (–18 °C), there was a crowd of 57, 167 fans.

RIVALRIES AND RIOTS

Geography and history. They're more than just subjects in school. Some people find them boring, but they're wrong! Geography and history are what make sports rivalries so intense! Scoring a big win over a nearby team you've been battling for years is always a great moment.

Saturday Night Battles

From 1938 until 1970, Montreal and Toronto were the only Canadian teams in the NHL. Fans all across Canada tuned in to their games, first on radio and later on television. During those 32 years, the Leafs and the Canadiens won the Stanley Cup 22 times! The Montreal-Toronto rivalry really took off during the 1946–47 season. That year marked the first time that the Canadiens and the Maple Leafs played each other for the Stanley Cup. They would meet again in 1951, 1959, 1960, and 1967.

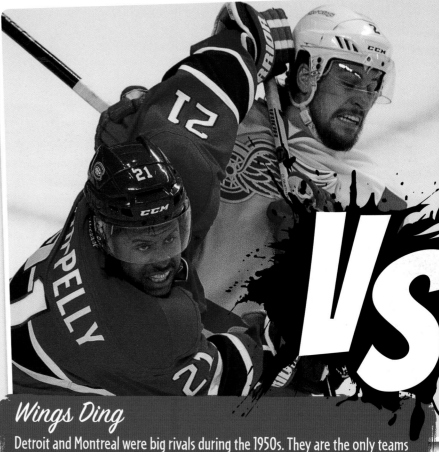

Wings Ding

Detroit and Montreal were big rivals during the 1950s. They are the only teams in hockey history to meet for the Stanley Cup three years in a row. The Red Wings won in 1954 and 1955, but the Canadiens came out on top in 1956.

Battle of Quebec

From 1979 through 1995, the Canadiens shared their home province with the Quebec Nordiques. When the two teams met—especially in the playoffs—it was known as "The Battle of Quebec." The Nordiques moved to Colorado in 1995 and became the Colorado Avalanche. The rivalry moved with them, particularly when former Montreal goaltender Patrick Roy was traded to Colorado in 1995, and the Avalanche went on to win the Stanley Cup.

The Richard Riot

"I went to a fight the other night and a hockey game broke out," is a joke told by comedian Rodney Dangerfield. It's no secret that fights were once very common in hockey, but did you know that a hockey fight caused a riot in Montreal? In March 1955, Montreal's Maurice Richard was suspended for the season and the playoffs for a violent on-ice attack on Boston Bruin Hal Laycoe. Laycoe had high-sticked Richard, causing a cut requiring stitches. Richard went after Laycoe and in his frenzy, punched a **linesman** and knocked him unconscious. Days later, NHL president Clarence Campbell handed Richard the suspension. Montreal fans were furious. They felt the suspension of their top player and the league's top scorer (up to that point) was too harsh. When Campbell attended the next Montreal home game, he was pelted with vegetables and punched by a fan. A tear-gas bomb was set off and the game was stopped. Fans then rioted outside, trashing businesses near the Forum. Up to 100 fans were arrested, but Richard's suspension stood. Montreal later lost the Stanley Cup to Detroit.

Glossary

blueliner Hockey slang for defense

embolism A blood clot or bubble of air that travels through a blood vessel and blocks the vessel

farm system Hockey teams that train young players to move up and play on professional teams

franchise A professional sports team

Great Depression An economic crisis from 1929 to 1939 where the stock market crashed, businesses closed, and many people were out of work

humiliation Feeling a loss of pride

iconic Something or someone that is idolized, admired or greatly loved

linesman An official who enforces the rules of the game. Linesmen watch for center line and blue line infractions.

reflexes Someone's abilities to perform actions automatically, without thinking

revered Someone or something that is honored or admired

stock market A place where big business stocks, or company shares, are traded

Further Reading

If you're a fan of the Montreal Canadiens, you may enjoy these books:

The Hockey Sweater by Roch Carrier. Tundra Books, 1984.

Center Ice: The Stanley Cup by Jaime Winters. Crabtree Publishing, 2015.

Montreal Canadiens: The Home Team by Holly Preston. Always Books Ltd, 2015.

Fever Season by Eric Zweig. Dundurn Press, 2009.

The Big Book of Hockey for Kids by Eric Zweig. Scholastic Canada 2013, 2017.

The Ultimate Book of Hockey Trivia for Kids by Eric Zweig. Scholastic Canada, 2015.

Websites to Check Out

The National Hockey League's official website: **www.nhl.com**

The Montreal Canadiens website: **www.nhl.com/canadiens**

The historical website of the Canadiens: **www.ourhistory.canadiens.com**

The Hockey Hall of Fame: **www.hhof.com**

Test Your HABS' Knowledge

1. In addition to the Canadiens, what other Montreal NHL team called the Forum home?

   a) Montreal Wonderers
   b) Montreal Crystals
   c) Montreal Maroons
   d) Montreal Roadrunners

2. Who was the first player to achieve 50 goals in one season and 500 career goals?

   a) Maurice Richard
   b) Jean Beliveau
   c) Bernie Geoffrion
   d) Bob Gainey

3. Which of these was **not** a nickname for Howie Morenz?

   a) The Stratford Streak
   b) The Fabulous Fast Guy
   c) The Canadian Comet
   d) The Mitchell Meteor

4. Who was the Canadiens speedster known as "The Roadrunner"?

   a) Georges Vezina
   b) Yvan Cournoyer
   c) Mario Trembley
   d) Larry Robinson

5. Which of these goalies won the Hart Trophy as NHL MVP?

   a) Jacques Plante
   b) José Théodore
   c) Carey Price
   d) All of the above

1. a) The Montreal Maroons; 2. a) Maurice Richard; 3. b) The Fabulous Fast Guy; 4. b) Yvan Cournoyer; 5. d) All of the above

Places to Go

If you're ever in Toronto, be sure to visit the Hockey Hall of Fame. If you're in Montreal, you can see a game at the Bell Centre or take a tour of the building. You may also want to eat, see a movie, go bowling, or play arcade games at the Montreal Forum. You can even see some artifacts from the team's history there.

About the Author

By the age of 10, Eric Zweig was already a budding sports fanatic who was filling his school news books with game reports instead of current events. He has been writing professionally about sports and sports history since 1985. Eric has written many sports books for adults and children, including the novels *Hockey Night in the Dominion of Canada* (Lester Publishing, 1992) and *Fever Season* (Dundurn Press, 2009). Eric is a member of the Society for International Hockey Research and the Society for American Baseball Research. Visit Eric's website at ericzweig.com

Index